15 Elf and Gnome Patterns for Carvers

Al Streetman

4880 Lower Valley Road, Atglen, PA 19310 USA

Acknowledgements

The following people helped make this book possible. I thank you all.

Jody Garrett, Woodcraft Supply Corp.: For all the help you give to us "starving artists", and for providing us with various carving tool samples for evaluation and consideration.

DecoArt: The paint samples were excellent, and satisfactory in all respects.

Woodcraft Supply Corp., Parkersburg, WV.: High-quality carving tools and supplies.

Royal Brush Mfg.,Inc.: Excellent quality paintbrushes at an affordable price.

Copyright © 1999 by Al Streetman
Library of Congress Catalog Card Number: 98-83140

Book Design by Anne Davidsen
Type set in Dom Bold/ Korinna

ISBN: 0-7643-0842-4
Printed in China

Published by Schiffer Publishing Ltd.
4880 Lower Valley Road
Atglen, PA 19310
Phone: (610) 593-1777
Fax: (610) 593-2002
E-mail: Schifferbk@aol.com
Please visit our web site catalog at
www.schifferbooks.com

This book may be purchased from the publisher.
Include $3.95 for shipping.
Please try your bookstore first.
We are interested in hearing from authors
with book ideas on related subjects.
You may write for a free catalog.

In Europe, Schiffer books are distributed by
Bushwood Books
6 Marksbury Rd.
Kew Gardens
Surrey TW9 4JF England
Phone: 44 (0)181 392-8585
Fax: 44 (0)181 392-9876
E-mail: Bushwd@aol.com

Table of Contents

Introduction

For those of you who may want to add some extra caricatures to your Christmas collection, but want something besides Santas, here is something you might want to try. Elves and gnomes are fun to carve, and since they resemble Santa-type people, many of the knife and gouge cuts are similar. The biggest difference is that you have much more latitude in the expressions you can give to the faces, and in the colors you use to paint the characters.

Elves and gnomes like to wear bright colors, and they like clothing with lots of decorations on it. If you have been looking for something to carve which lets you exercise your "artistic license", then read on.

We will go through one project in full detail, from carving, to painting, to mounting the elf on a base. The other patterns are similar, so once you go through the project, the same techniques presented can be applied to create more elves and gnomes.

Some of you may observe that my carving project is not as complex or detailed as you might carve it, but there is a method to my madness! In this book, as in my previous books, I have tried to design a project that would yield a nice result, yet not be so complex or involved that the *beginning* wood carver would not be able to accomplish it. I want to reach as many wood carvers as possible, and share the joy of carving with them. As the beginners gain more experience, they can add additional details as desired.

Except for the actual carving project, I have not included specific carving instructions. I have found that each carver has his or her own style, and each has their preference for which tool to use in a particular area, or to achieve a particular effect.

Rather than giving a vague instruction such as "use a small gouge", I have listed the particular size tool I used in the different steps of the carving project, as we move through each step. This is more for the benefit of the beginning carver than the experienced one. If you don't have these particular sizes of gouges or tools, use something similar.

Each pattern in this book shows all the component pieces needed to make that particular carving. All the pieces are in scale to each other, so if you enlarge or reduce a pattern, the pattern pieces will still be in the right proportion to each other. If you desire a larger or smaller version, simply enlarge or shrink the pattern on a photocopying machine. (In the "Tips" section, I explain reducing and enlarging patterns with a copying machine if this is new to you).

On the patterns, you will notice an arrow with a "G" superimposed over it. This arrow indicates the recommended grain direction of the wood in relation to the pattern, in order to make carving that particular piece as easy as possible.

I use Basswood whenever possible, but any soft wood such as Jelutong, clear Spruce, or Sugar/White Pine will work equally well. If possible, use a bandsaw with a 1/8" or 3/16" blade to cut out the pattern pieces. The bandsaw will allow you to release the rough version of the pattern from the block of wood faster than trying to use a coping saw or other means to cut out the pattern.

General Notes

1. Trace the pattern pieces, or make a copy of them on a photocopying machine. Glue the pattern you copied or traced to some heavy paper such as poster paper or a manila file folder. When the glue is dry, cut out the pattern. This method will prevent you from ruining the master patterns in your book.

2. Lay your pattern on the wood, trace the outline of it, and saw it out. *Pay close attention to any recommended grain directions indicated on the pattern pieces!*

3. You should now have a rough blank ready to be carved.

4. Use your own techniques and style to bring the carving to the finished stage.

5. In the "Tips" section, there is information describing hand carving separately from the arm, if you are not familiar with this technique.

6. *I recommend that you read the entire book before starting the project.* This will help you see where we are going, and will help alert you to carving techniques that may be unfamiliar. In the section where we paint the project, you may see an area or detail that might not have been clear to you in the carving section. Reading the entire book through before beginning the project will help you identify any such areas, and may help eliminate frustration at a later time. Remember, if we carve it, we will paint it, so you will see everything at least twice.

7. If you see a pattern that you wish to carve, *pay close attention to the pattern page.* Although I submit all the patterns to the publisher full-size, it may be necessary for a certain number of them to be reduced in size in order to meet the page requirements of the book. If a particular pattern has been reduced in size, it will be so indicated somewhere on the pattern. The information I included in the TIPS section concerning enlarging/reducing will tell you how to get the pattern back to full-size, or any other size you may wish to make it.

Project Carving Tools

1/8" V gouge

1/4" V gouge

1/4" #8 U gouge

Fixed blade (Bütz) carving and detail knives—General wood removal and details such as eye carving.

For those of you who are not familiar with the type of cuts different gouges make, or how large the cut is for a specific size of gouge, I have included a Gouge Reference Chart in this book. If you want to use a different gouge other than one which I used, this chart will be helpful in determining what type of gouge you might want to try.

Gouge Reference Charts

(Reprinted with the permission of Woodcraft Supply Corp.)

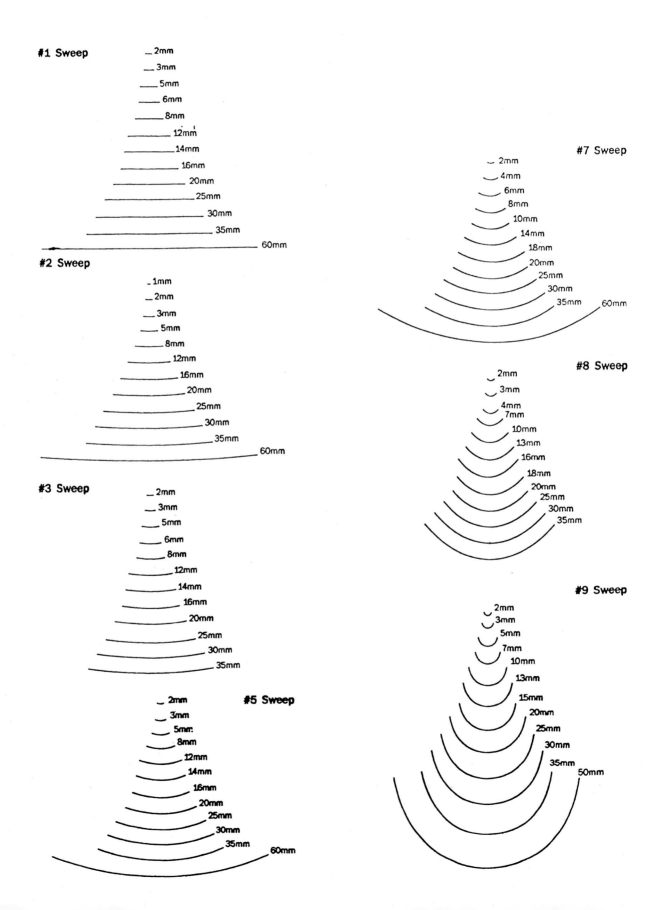

#1 Sweep
- 2mm
- 3mm
- 5mm
- 6mm
- 8mm
- 12mm
- 14mm
- 16mm
- 20mm
- 25mm
- 30mm
- 35mm
- 60mm

#2 Sweep
- 1mm
- 2mm
- 3mm
- 5mm
- 8mm
- 12mm
- 16mm
- 20mm
- 25mm
- 30mm
- 35mm
- 60mm

#3 Sweep
- 2mm
- 3mm
- 5mm
- 6mm
- 8mm
- 12mm
- 14mm
- 16mm
- 20mm
- 25mm
- 30mm
- 35mm

#5 Sweep
- 2mm
- 3mm
- 5mm
- 8mm
- 12mm
- 14mm
- 16mm
- 20mm
- 25mm
- 30mm
- 35mm
- 60mm

#7 Sweep
- 2mm
- 4mm
- 6mm
- 8mm
- 10mm
- 14mm
- 18mm
- 20mm
- 25mm
- 30mm
- 35mm
- 60mm

#8 Sweep
- 2mm
- 3mm
- 4mm
- 7mm
- 10mm
- 13mm
- 16mm
- 18mm
- 20mm
- 25mm
- 30mm
- 35mm

#9 Sweep
- 2mm
- 3mm
- 5mm
- 7mm
- 10mm
- 13mm
- 15mm
- 20mm
- 25mm
- 30mm
- 35mm
- 50mm

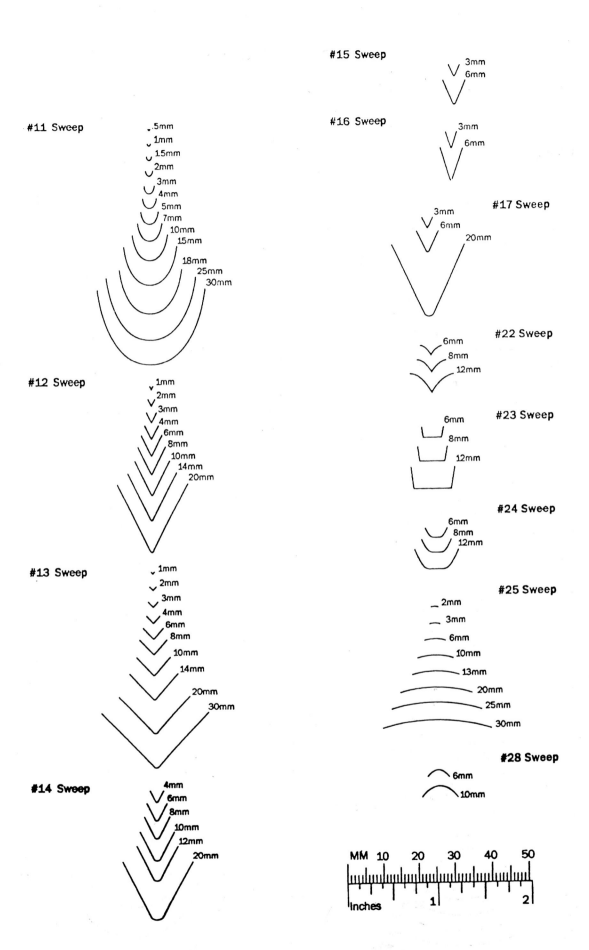

#11 Sweep
.5mm
1mm
1.5mm
2mm
3mm
4mm
5mm
7mm
10mm
15mm
18mm
25mm
30mm

#12 Sweep
1mm
2mm
3mm
4mm
6mm
8mm
10mm
14mm
20mm

#13 Sweep
1mm
2mm
3mm
4mm
6mm
8mm
10mm
14mm
20mm
30mm

#14 Sweep
4mm
6mm
8mm
10mm
12mm
20mm

#15 Sweep
3mm
6mm

#16 Sweep
3mm
6mm

#17 Sweep
3mm
6mm
20mm

#22 Sweep
6mm
8mm
12mm

#23 Sweep
6mm
8mm
12mm

#24 Sweep
6mm
8mm
12mm

#25 Sweep
2mm
3mm
6mm
10mm
13mm
20mm
25mm
30mm

#28 Sweep
6mm
10mm

MM 10 20 30 40 50
Inches 1 2

Carving Tips

1. Here are some different ways to carve eyes:

   A. Quilt Pin Method: I often use various sizes of plastic-head quilting pins to make eyes. Mark where you want the eyes to be on the finished carving. Using a drill and bit that is slightly larger than the pin head you are going to use, make a hole for each eye.

   Using wire cutters, snip off the pin head, leaving about 1/4" of the pin attached to the head.

   Insert the pin head into the eye socket, with the pin end going in first. Use a nail set to seat the head into the hole until only a small orb protrudes. This gives a fairly realistic eye without causing too much effort on your part. For extra detail, remove a triangular-shaped piece of wood from the sides of the pin head. This will make a very realistic eye when it is painted.

   B. Punch Method: A second way to create eyes the easy way is to use carver's eye punches. Select the size eye punch you want to use, based on the size of the eye sockets you have made. Push the eye punch against the socket firmly and rotate it. After making both eyes, remove triangular-shaped pieces of wood from the corners to give more detail. Use your knife, if necessary, to smooth and round off the eyeball.

   C. Football Method: A more realistic way to make eyes is to first carve the eye sockets to form about a 90° angle, so when you view the head from the side, the angle will form a "V" going into the face. Lightly sketch in a football-shaped eye in each socket, such that the top half of the football is on the upper half of the socket, and the lower half of the football is on the lower half of the socket. When you sketch in the footballs, make the outside ends lower than the inside ends. Using the tip of your knife, score the football outline to a depth of about 1/16". Now use the tip of your knife to remove triangular-shaped pieces of wood from the left and right corner of each eye. This will leave a small section of wood inside each football, which will be the eyeball. Use your knife to round off and smooth the eyeball. You can vary the way you remove the triangular-shaped corners, if you want the eyes to be looking more to one side, rather than straight ahead.

   D. Mound Method: The most realistic way to make eyes is to first rough carve the nose so it is standing out from the face. Next, sketch a circle or oval on each side of the nose to represent where the eye mounds will be located. Using a smaller "V" gouge, such as a 1/8" size, or your knife tip, go around the circles or ovals so the mounds will be defined, and separated from the face area. Use your knife to round the sharp edges of the mounds, and the face area around the mounds.

   Divide the mounds into thirds by sketching two curved horizontal lines across each one, making sure that the lines join at each corner of the mound. Look at your own eyes in a mirror to see what I mean here. Using your knife tip, score each horizontal line about 1/16" deep. Working from the *center* of the eye mound, use your knife tip to shave *upward* toward the top horizontal line, and *downward* toward the bottom horizontal line. This will make the eyelids stand out from the eyeball area. Finally, remove small triangular pieces of wood from each corner of the eye, so the eyeball will be rounded from left to right, as well as top to bottom.

   Changing the size and shape of the mounds, and the spacing between the horizontal lines, will allow you to achieve many effects and expressions on your carvings.

   One last thing concerning eyes: Don't get upset if you discover that you have carved one eye smaller or at a different angle than the other eye. This "accident" may work to your advantage. It will lend an interesting variation to the carving, and no one has to know you didn't do it that way on purpose!

2. When buying wood, whether it be Basswood, Spruce, or some other type, try to pick the *lightest* pieces. They tend to have less fat and sap in them, so they are *easier* to carve.

3. An easy way to help determine where you want to place some wrinkles and folds in the arms, torso, and legs is to observe and note where the wood grain changes direction as you are carving. Usually in the crook of an elbow or behind the knees, you will notice that wood "fuzzies" try to appear, no matter how carefully you carve or how sharp your knife is. That is because the wood grain direction is changing, and in one direction or the other, you are trying to carve against the grain, thus the "fuzzies" appear. These spots are perfect candidates for wrinkles and folds, made with a large "V" tool or by cutting wedges out with your knife. As a beginning carver, if you do nothing more than add a few cuts in these areas, you will be amazed at the difference in the way the carving looks. With experience, you will start noticing other places to add wrinkles and folds.

4. For those of you who have never had much practice enlarging or reducing patterns, or being able to calculate how much enlargement or reduction you need to select on the photocopying machine, here are some general guidelines.

   Let's say you have a pattern that shows a side profile requiring 2" thick wood, and you want to make the pattern larger so it will fit on 3" thick wood. Use the following formula to calculate what percentage enlargement to select on the copier:

**[New Dimension Desired
÷ Present Dimension] x100 = %**

Using our example, this would work out as follows:

$$[3" \div 2"] \times 100 = \mathbf{150\%}.$$

Going the other way, let's say you have a pattern that shows a 2" side profile, and you want to reduce it down so it will fit on a piece of 1-3/4" thick wood. Using the same formula, it works out as follows:

$$[1.75" \div 2"] \times 100 = \mathbf{87.5\%}.$$

If the machine you are using won't go large enough or small enough to get the job done on the first try, additional steps may be required. Go ahead and make your first copy using the largest enlargement or reduction setting you can select. Measure the *new* dimensions on your copy, which will now be your *present dimension*, then use the same formula as before to calculate how much additional enlargement or reduction is needed to get the pattern to the size you desired it to be.

5. When making separate hands that are going to be holding an object, it is easiest if you first cut out the top profile of the hand, drill a hole large enough for the object to fit through, then saw out the side profile of the hand. This procedure will help prevent the hand from splitting when you drill it.

6. For those patterns where the hands are to be carved separately, the following instructions may be used if you are not familiar with this method of hand carving:

A. Lay out the top view of the hands on a piece of 3/4" thick basswood. Leave a short section of wood at the rear of each hand when you lay out the pattern. This section will serve as a handle while you carve and shape the hands, and will form the wrist pegs in a later step. Saw out the top profile of the hands.

B. Now, using the top set of hands in the Hand Studies as a reference, sketch in the side profile of the hands, then saw them out. You now should have two hands that will require very little work to finish.

C. Sketch in the thumbs. Remove wood from each hand using a knife or a **#7 10mm "U" gouge**, so the thumbs are well-defined, then round off the sharp edges of the thumbs.

D. Draw a line in the middle of the finger section to divide it in half. Now draw lines to divide each of these sections in half. You should now have four fingers defined, all approximately equal.

E. Using a 1/8" **"V" gouge**, go over these lines so the fingers will be separated. As an option, to add further detail without too much pain on your part, use a bandsaw, scroll saw or coping saw to carefully saw along these lines. Use your knife to remove any fuzzy wood caused by the saw cuts, and to remove any sharp edges still remaining on the hands. At this point, if you do nothing

else, you will have two hands that will look perfectly good once they are painted. Experienced carvers may add more detailing as they desire, such as knuckles and wrinkles on the finger joints.

F. Using your knife, trim down the sections of wood protruding from the rear of the hands, so as to form a "wrist" or "pin" that will fit snugly into the holes you drilled earlier in the arms. When done properly, the hand should appear to be coming out of the sleeve. This method allows you to turn the hands in various directions, so your carvings will appear more lifelike.

General Painting Suggestions and Paintbrush Recommendations

I have included some *suggested* colors and paint brushes for all patterns. If you have a preference for a different color scheme, by all means use it. After all, it's your carving, and you can paint it any way you desire.

I have also listed the colors produced by DecoArt and their identification numbers, which I have found to be suitable for painting these carvings. I have used these colors, and the results were excellent. I hope this will help minimize your confusion when trying to sort through the maze of paint brands and colors at your hobby or craft store.

The best paintbrushes I have found, for the money, are made by the Royal Brush Mfg. Company. They come in a wide assortment of sizes and shapes, are durable, and most important are affordable. In general, here are the ones I use and recommend for painting your carvings.

Royal Golden Taklon series 250 Round, size 0 and 00: Details such as eyes and other small areas.

Royal Golden Taklon series 170 Cat's Tongue, size 2 and 4: Large areas.

Royal Golden Taklon series 150 Short Shader, size 2 and 4: Blending colors. (For example when blending a "blush" color into the flesh color on faces, hands, etc.)

You may have heard and read this a million times, but when painting your carvings, keep the word THIN in mind. What you want to do is stain the wood to give it some color and life, but you don't want the paint so thick that it covers up the beauty of the wood. NOTE: When painting faces and hair, I generally use a little thicker mixture of paint than I use on the rest of the carving. I want the face to be a bit more intense than the rest of the carving, since the head and face is what sets most of the mood for the carving.

Suggested Colors

Titanium White #DA1 (Eyes)
Light Buttermilk #DA164 (Hair, beards, eyebrows)
Fleshtone #DA78 (Skin areas)
Blush Flesh #DA110 ("Blushing" effects)
Baby Blue #DA42 (Eyes)
Lamp Black #DA67 (Eyes)
Napthol Red #DA104 (Hats)
True Blue #DA36 (Coats)
Emperor's Gold #DA148 (Buttons, trim on coats)
Yellow Ochre #DA8 (Shirts)
Mink Tan #DA92 (Trousers)
Burnt Umber #DA64 (Shoe and boot soles)
Red Iron Oxide #DA96 (Upper part of shoes, boots)
Oak Antiquing Gel #DS30 ("Aging" the finished carving)
Clear Satin Varnish #DS15 (Sealing the finished carving)

Remember: These are only a few of the many colors you can use for your carvings. Should you have other color preferences, use them. Don't be afraid to get wild and experiment with all sorts of color combinations. For those of you (like me), who have difficulty trying to decide which colors work well together, most hobby and art supply stores sell inexpensive color wheels which will show you colors that work together, and colors that oppose each other. I have listed a few combinations here, for illustrative purposes:

Main Color	Contrast Color
Red	Green
Orange	Blue
Yellow	Violet

A good color wheel will not only show you main and contrast colors, it will also show colors that blend.

"Antiquing" The Project

Once the paint is dry, you may want to "age" your carving with an antiquing product in order to help tone down the colors a bit. I have had excellent results using antiquing gels made by DecoArt. These are available at hobby and craft stores. They come in various colors, so you can create different effects.

Brush a coat of antiquing gel on the wood, then wipe it off using a damp rag or sponge. It is your option how much you wipe off. After the antiquing is dry, I like to finish my carvings with a coat of brush-on acrylic varnish. DecoArt also makes an excellent varnish. I prefer the one that leaves a Satin finish. This particular finish is not too flat nor too glossy, but leaves a "soft" look to the completed carving. I usually put a coat of varnish on the face, hands and other flesh areas *before* I antique the carving. This will prevent these areas from absorbing too much antiquing color.

Carving the Project

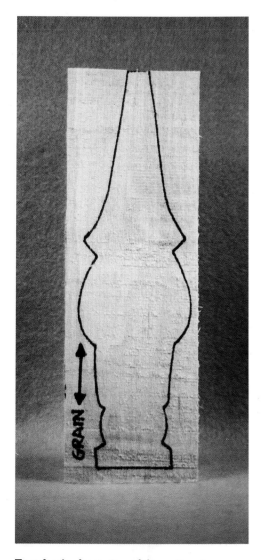

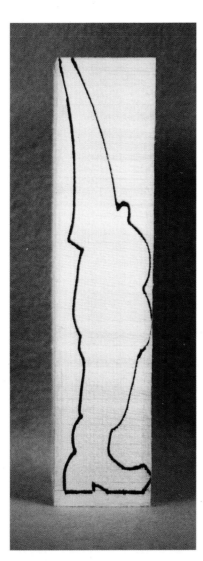

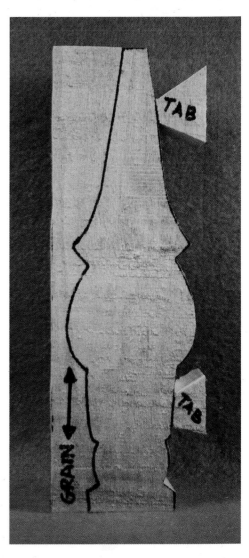

Transfer the front view of the pattern to an appropriately-sized piece of wood. Pay close attention to the indicated direction of the wood grain on the pattern. By having the grain run vertically through the head and body, your carving experience will be more pleasant, and adding details to the carving later will be much easier.

Next, transfer the side view of the pattern to the wood.

Saw away excess wood from the left side of the pattern, but leave a few "tabs", as I have done here. These tabs will help hold the wood level when we saw out the side profile in a moment.

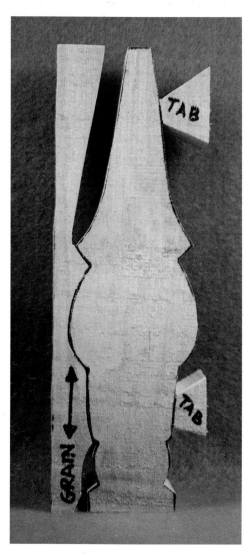

Make saw cuts on the right side of the body as shown here, but DO NOT cut the wood completely away from the body at this time. (We need to keep the wood on this side of the body intact until we saw out the side profile).

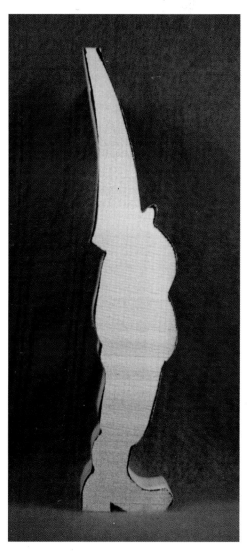

Lay the wood on its edge and saw out the side profile *completely*. Here is where you will appreciate the purpose of the tabs you left in place earlier.

Next, lay the wood flat again and saw away *all* the excess wood from the body, including the tabs. Now we are ready to begin roughing out the arms and other features. Grab a big cup of coffee or other refreshment and let's get busy!

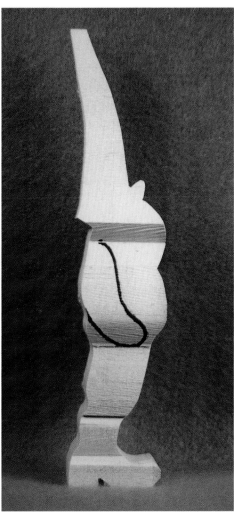

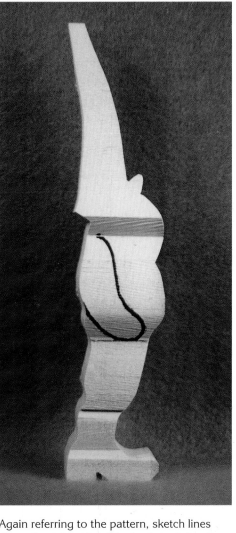

Referring to the pattern, sketch a line down the front right side of the body to define and separate the right arm from the body.

Again referring to the pattern, sketch lines down the right side of the body to define the width of the right arm and hand. Then, using the tip of your knife, incise the lines approximately 1/8" deep in order to create some "stop cuts" which will help control our wood removal.

We are going to remove the darkened sections of wood. You may use your knife, a flat gouge, or any other tool that works best for you. Work from the *front* of the body back to the arm, slicing away the wood. You will have to keep incising the lines and shaving away wood until the section is removed.

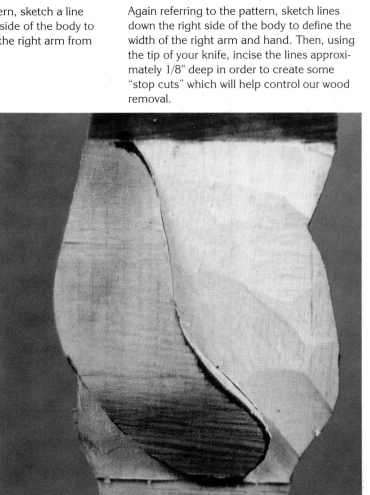

Here is how it looks after a few cuts...

13

...and here is how it looks with all the darkened wood removed, from the front view. At this time, don't worry about the head and beard areas. We are going to work on them later. For now, let's concentrate on removing excess wood from the arms in order to give us better access to the rest of the body.

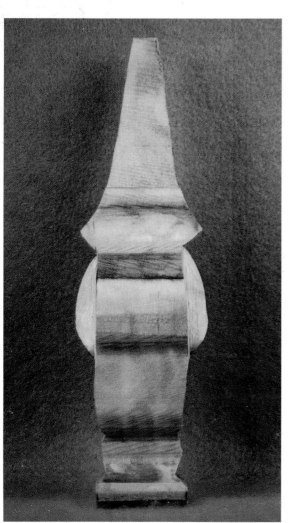

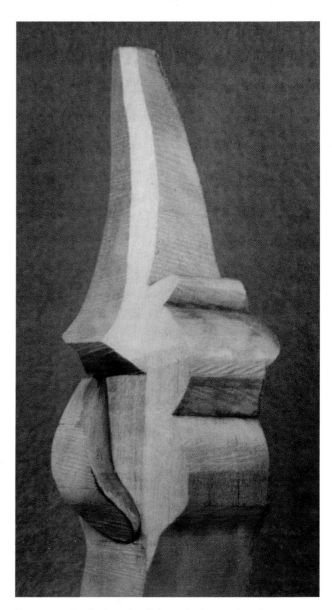

Using your knife, knock off the right front edge, from approximately the bottom of the hands, all the way up through the beard, head and hat, at about a 45° angle...

Apply these same techniques to the left side to define and separate the left arm from the body, to arrive at this stage.

...and do the same thing on the right rear sharp edge.

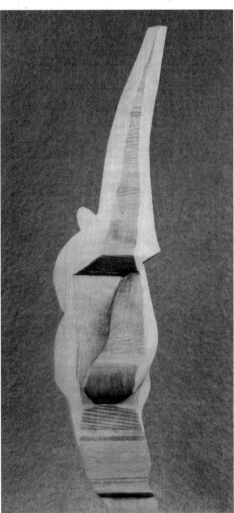

Repeat this process for the two sharp edges on the left side of the body.

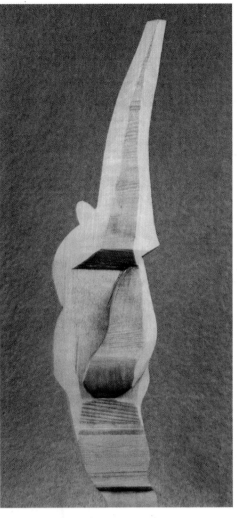

Now that the four severe sharp edges have been removed, the upper body has taken on an octagonal shape, and we now have 8 smaller sharp edges. Using your knife, shave away these eight sharp edges again at about a 45° angle (but on a smaller scale), and the upper part of the body should be round enough for now.

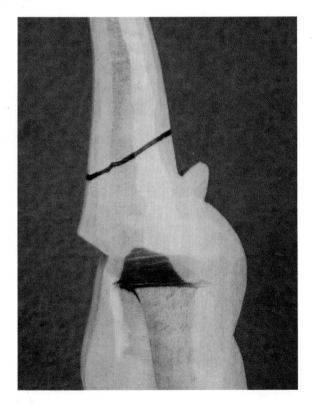

Sketch a line around the head to define the separation between the hat and hair, then incise this line about 1/8" deep with the tip of your knife.

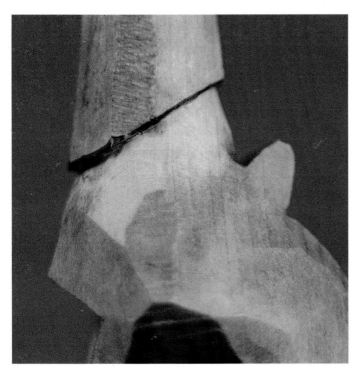

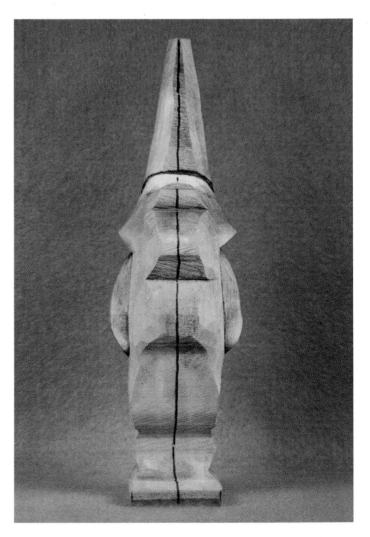

Working from the bottom of the head, use your knife to shave *up* toward the line you just incised, all the way around the head. This will make the face and hair appear as if they are going into the hat, and also gets our detailing process started.

At this time, to help maintain symmetry as we carve the face and other details, sketch a line all the way down the front and back of the body to indicate the approximate centerline.

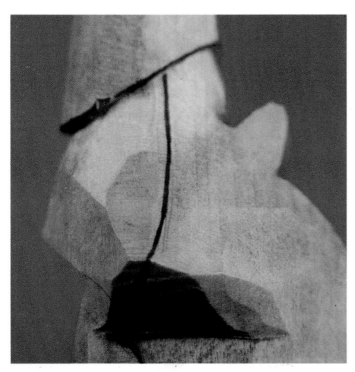

Sketch a line as shown to indicate the separation between the hair and beard on the right side of the face. Incise this line about 1/8" deep with your knife.

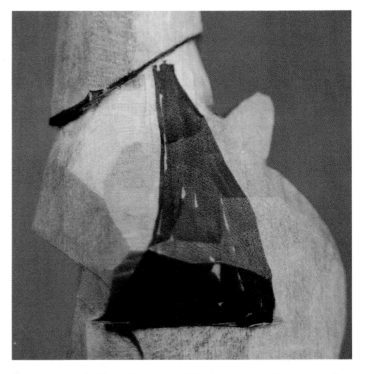

Now, use your knife to shave away the darkened section of wood.

Next, use your knife to round off the front edge of the hair on the right side.

Keep removing wood in this area until the beard and face are at the same level, as shown here.

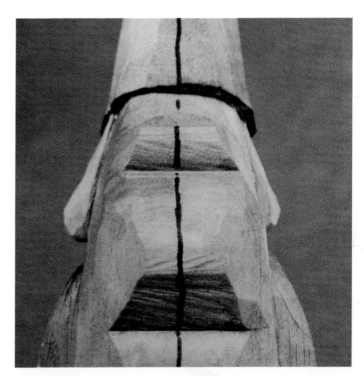

Now repeat these preliminary steps on the left side of the face and hair, to arrive at this point.

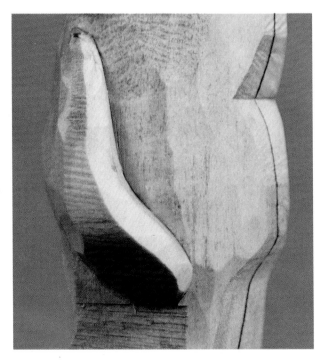

Before going any further with the face, let's finish the arms and hands so we'll have a better idea about where we want the lower beard line to be placed in a later step. First, use your knife to knock off the two sharp edges of the right arm at about a 45° angle.

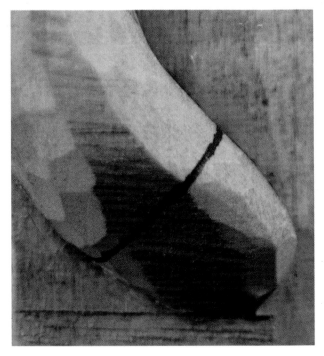

Sketch a line to define the separation of the hand and sleeve, then incise this line about 1/8" deep with the tip of your knife.

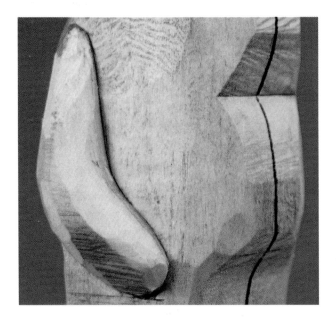

Now, use your knife to remove the new sharp edges you just created.

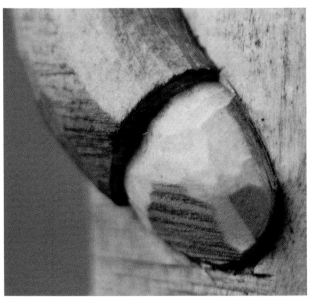

Working from the bottom of the hand, shave up *toward* the sleeve to remove a layer of wood and make the hand appear as if it is going up into the sleeve.

Next, clip off the top and bottom rear edges of the hand at about a 45° angle, to form a slight "wrist".

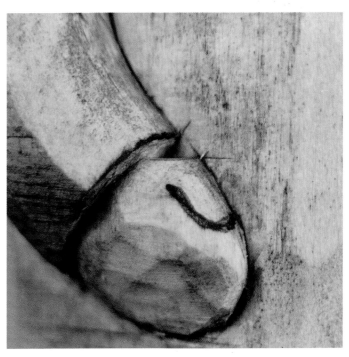

Sketch a line to indicate the separation of the thumb and fingers, and incise the line about 1/8" deep with your knife tip.

Use your knife to remove any remaining sharp edges on the hand.

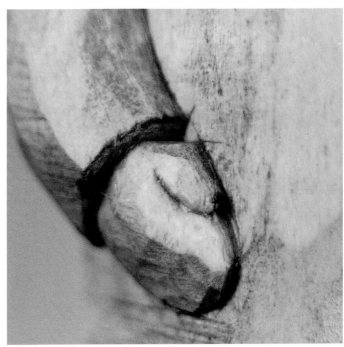

Using your knife tip, shave *upward* on the finger portion of the hand. This will remove a small amount of wood, causing the thumb to stand out from the finger portion. Then lightly shave the sharp edge from the thumb so it will be slightly rounded off.

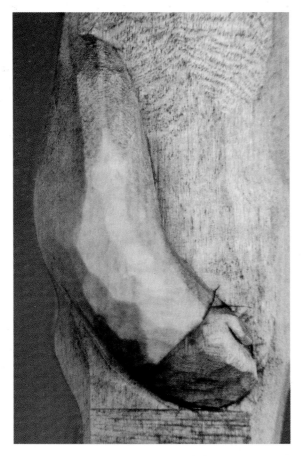

Look over this arm and hand, and if there are any areas that have been untouched by your knife, lightly shave away wood from these areas. This will "surface" the entire arm and hand, removing any saw marks and making the wood more receptive to painting later.

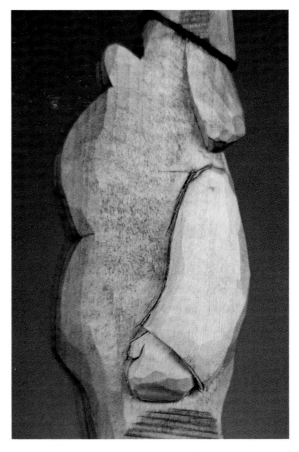

Repeat this entire process on the left arm to bring it to a finished state. NOTE: Because I designed this project so it could be accomplished by beginners and less experienced carvers, I purposely have not included finger detailing on the hands. More experienced carvers may add as much detailing as they desire to bring the hands to a more "finished" state.

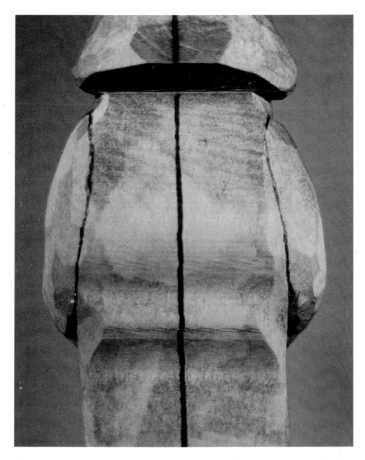

Sketch lines as shown in the rear, to define the separation of the left and right arms from the coat.

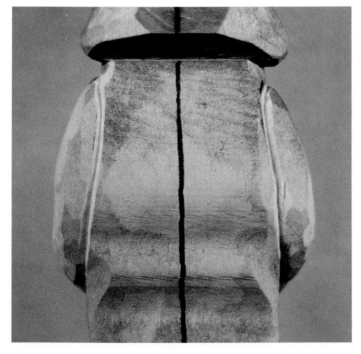

Using your knife, or a **1/4" V gouge**, remove wood along these lines so that a shallow "V" channel is formed, to finish defining the arms in the rear.

Now, use your knife to remove any sharp edges from the hair in the rear. Repeat as necessary until no severe sharp edges remain.

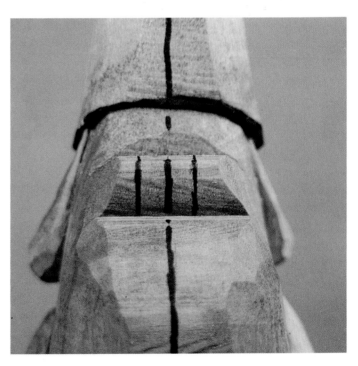

I know you can't stand the suspense any longer, so let's get serious about putting a face on this guy. First, sketch some lines to define the width of the nose. Leave the nose a little wider than you think it should be for now. You can always slim it down later if it looks too big, but it is real difficult to make it wider once the wood is gone! Then, incise these lines with your knife, about 1/8" deep.

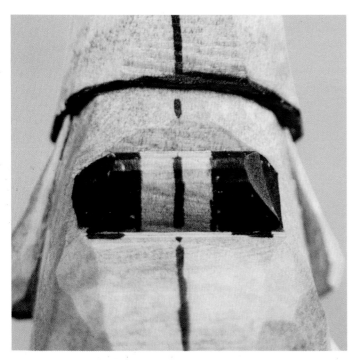

We want to remove the darkened sections of wood with a knife or flat gouge in order to make the nose stand out from the face.

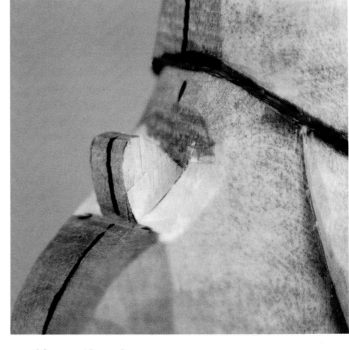

...and from a side angle.

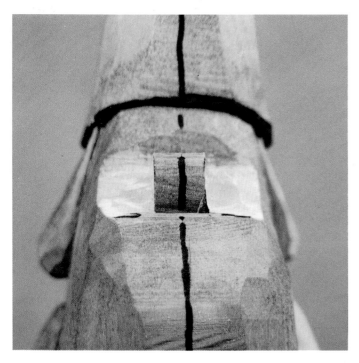

Keep incising and shaving away wood as necessary until you get the darkened sections removed, similar to what you see in this front view...

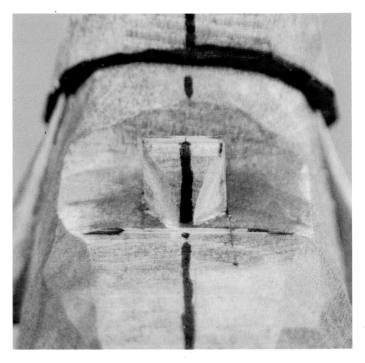

Now clip off the *lower* corners of the nose at about a 45° angle.

Then do the same thing on the top corners of the nose.

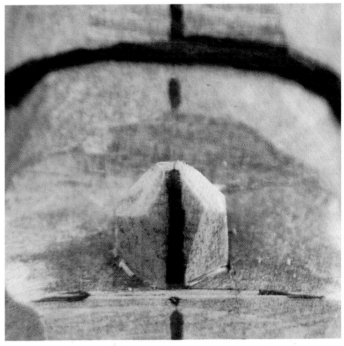

Next, clip off the two sharp edges on the front of the nose at about a 45° angle.

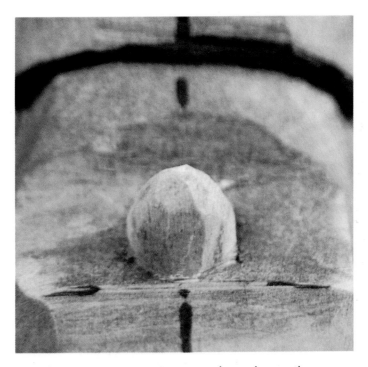

Now, shave away any remaining severe sharp edges on the nose, and the nose should be fairly round.

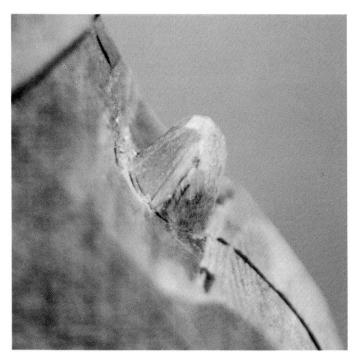

To create a nostril flare, scoop *in* and *up* on both sides of the nose, using the tip of your knife.

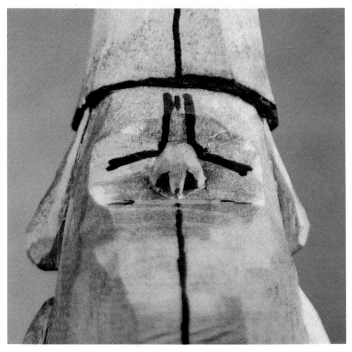

To start the eye area, sketch some lines as shown. Incise these lines about 1/8" deep with your detail knife.

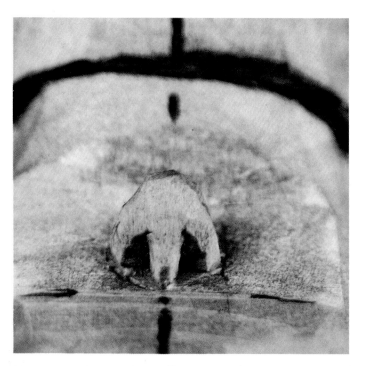

Now, use your detail knife tip to remove two "V"-shaped chips of wood from the bottom of the nose to simulate nostril openings.

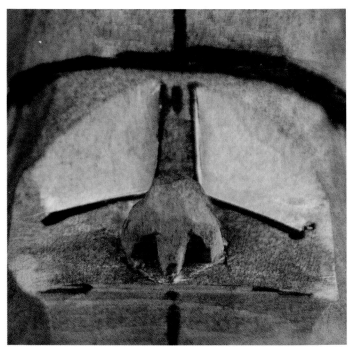

Shave *in* and *up* with your detail knife, working from the outer edges of the face in toward the nose, to form the eye areas as shown in this front view...

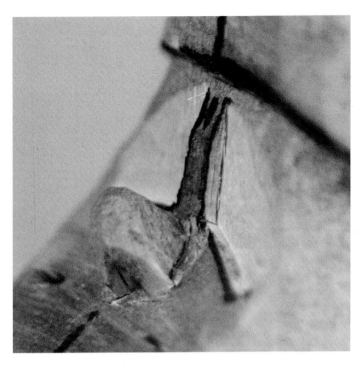

...and in this angle view.

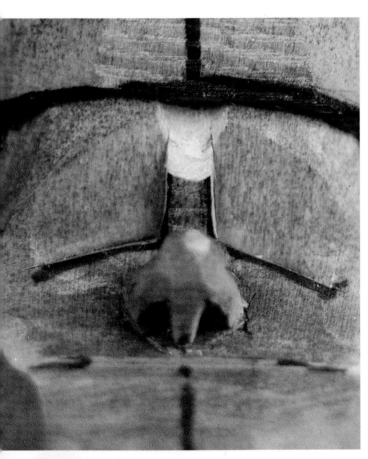

Using a 1/4" **No. 8 "U" gouge**, remove a section of wood at the top of the nose to separate the eyes and form the division between the eyebrows.

Now, sketch in two eyes as shown, and incise the lines all the way around about 1/8" deep with the tip of your detail knife. These big eyes will give the little guy a real friendly look when painted, and they are fun to carve.

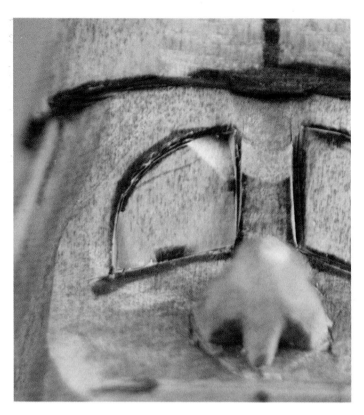

Using the tip of your detail knife, clip the two inside corners and the lower outside corner of the right eye, at about a 45° angle, and remove the small chips of wood.

Repeat this process for the other eye.

Now use your detail knife to remove the remaining edges of the eye at about the same angle. Then round off any sharp edges that may still be there, and the eye is done.

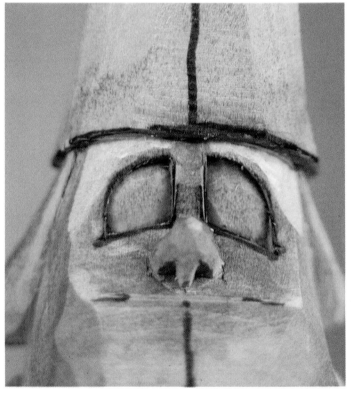

To form the eyebrows, use your detail knife and with an upward scooping motion, remove a small amount of wood above and along the sides of the eyes.

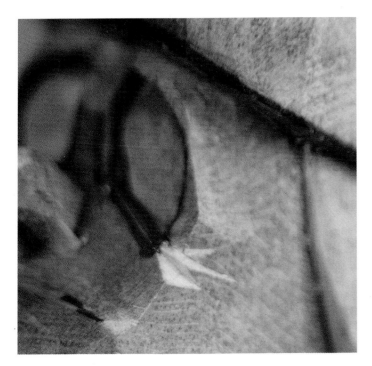

Last, let's put a few wrinkles in the corner of each eye to add a bit more character to our little fella. With your knife or **1/8" "V" gouge**, cut in a few "V"-shaped wrinkles as shown here.

Sketch in the cheek lines, and incise them about 1/8" deep with your detail knife tip.

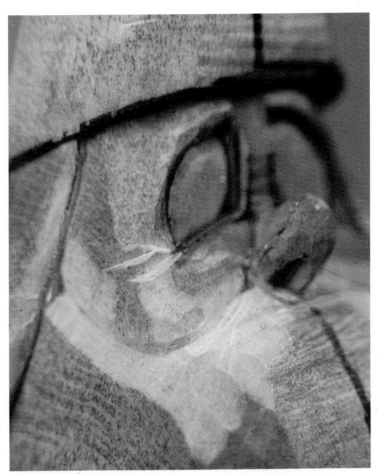

Using your knife shave *down* toward the line, and shave *up* toward the line, so a "V"-shaped channel is formed to separate the cheeks from the beard and mustache. Then, round off any sharp edges remaining on the cheeks.

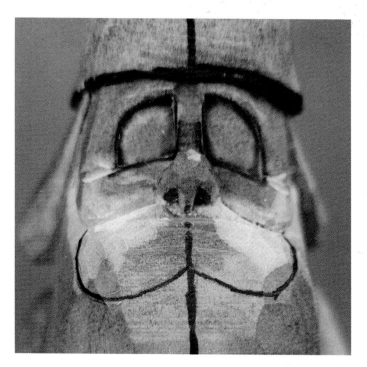

We are going to put a happy little mustache on this guy, so sketch in some lines as shown. Then, incise the lines about 1/8" deep with your knife.

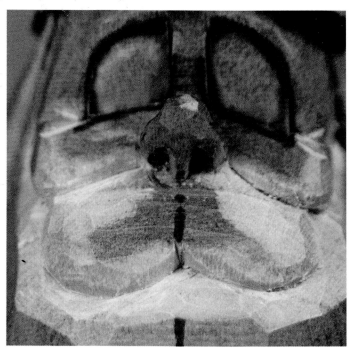

Shave *down* toward the lines, and *up* toward the lines you just incised, to make the mustache stand out. Then, round off any remaining sharp edges on the mustache.

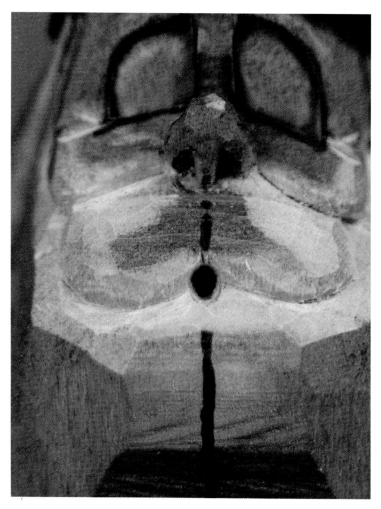

To form a mouth, use a 1/8" nail punch, or a drill with a 1/8" bit, and make a hole as shown.

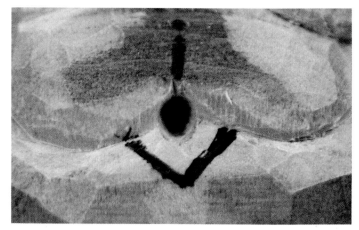

The bottom lip is made by first sketching some lines and incising them lightly with your detail knife.

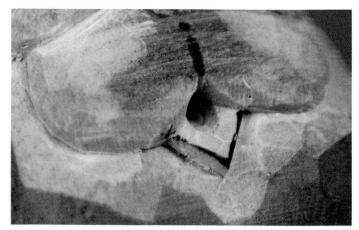

Shave *up* toward the lines to remove a small amount of wood and make the lip section stand out.

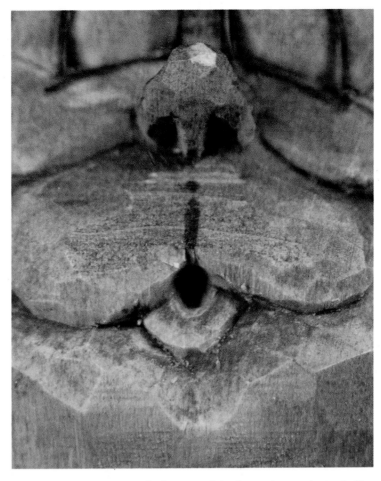

Clip off the sharp point at the bottom of the lip section, and round off any remaining sharp corners.

Referring to the pattern, sketch a line to define the beard, then incise the line with your knife as we have been doing on other steps.

As before, shave toward the incision from both directions in order to make the beard stand out from the body.

To add some texture to the hair and beard, yet maintain the "bold" carving look, I have used a **1/4" #8 "U" gouge** to cut in some details.

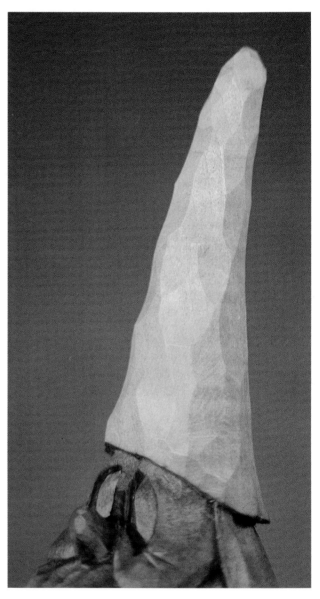

Now that we are done with the face and head detailing, let's finish rounding off the hat so we can work on the rest of the body. Using your knife as before, keep removing the sharp edges from the hat until it looks something like this. Quit when you are satisfied, but leave some of the knife planes and facets intact.

Draw lines to define the coat in front....

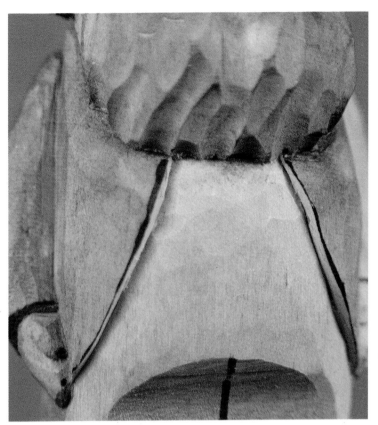

Shave back toward these lines in the front, working from the center of the chest *outward* and from the legs *upward*, until the wood comes free. This will give the coat some definition, and make it stand out from the body, as shown here...

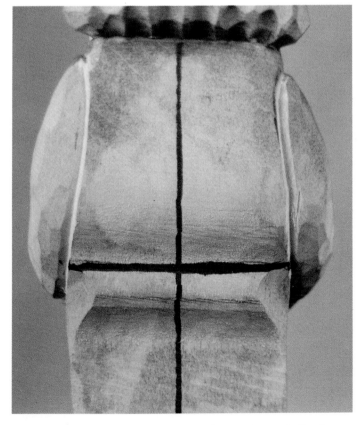

And around the back side. Incise these lines with your knife about 1/8" deep.

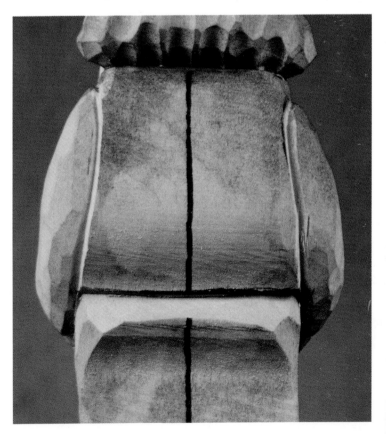

...and in this rear view.

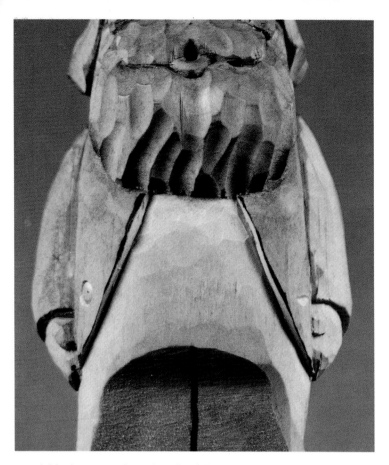

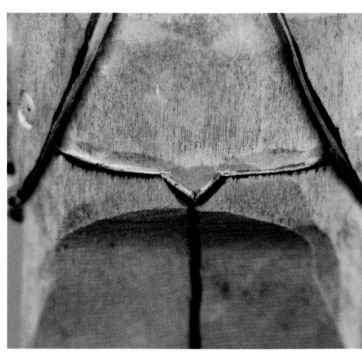

Add a button to the right side of the coat using a small nailset or eye punch, and use a **1/8" "V" gouge** to make a buttonhole on the left side of the coat.

Incise the lines lightly with your knife, and shave down *toward* them removing small amounts of wood. This will give the appearance of the shirt being tucked into the pants, like so.

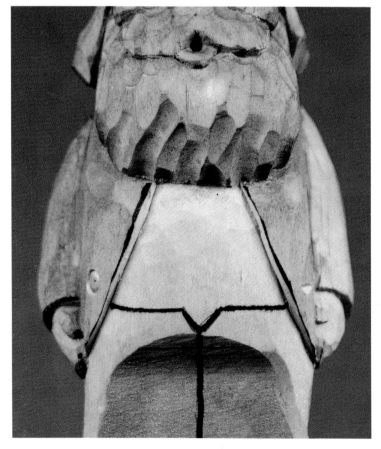

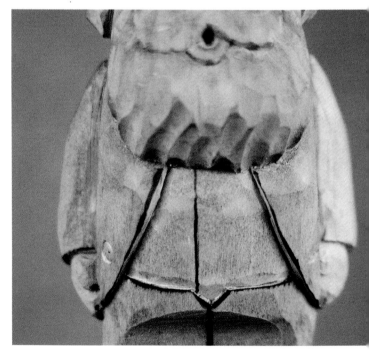

Sketch the top of the pants.

Sketch a line down the front of the shirt and lightly incise it with your knife.

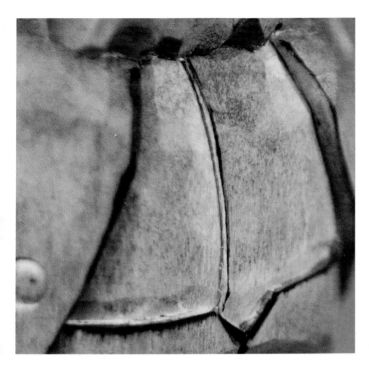

Working from the right side of the body *toward* the line you just incised, shave away a small amount of wood, so the right side of the shirt will be slightly lower than the left side.

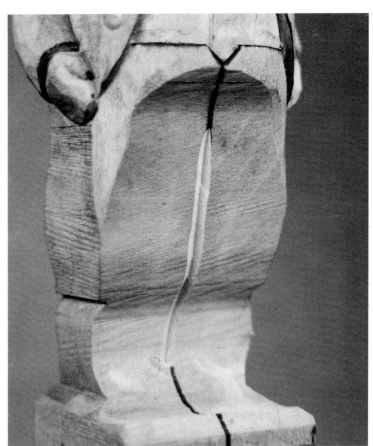

If necessary, re-draw the center line up the legs in front, and in the back. Go over these lines with your knife tip or **1/8" "V" gouge** to make a "V" channel and define the leg separation in front...

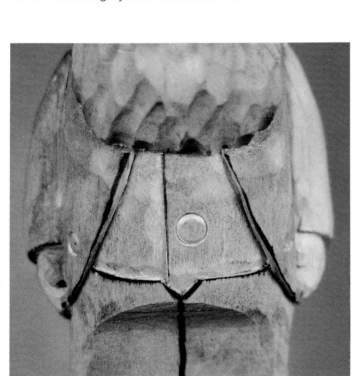

Use a 1/4" eye punch or nail set to put one large button on the left side of the shirt. I find that one big button looks better on carvings of this nature than several smaller ones.

...and in back. We will get the shoe separation defined in a later step.

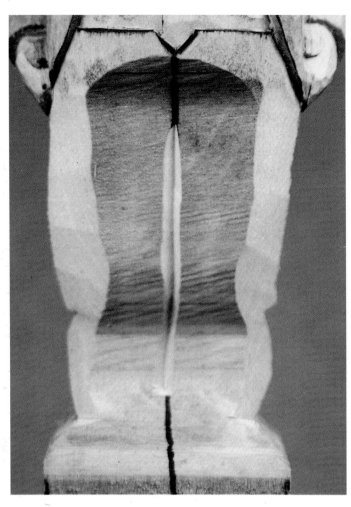

Use your knife to knock off all four sharp edges on the legs and stockings (front and rear), but leave the shoes alone for now.

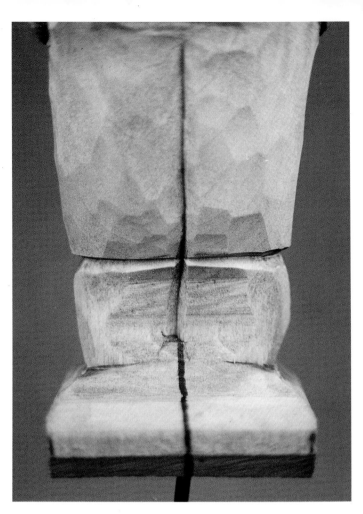

Sketch a line around the legs to indicate the separation of the pants and stockings. Follow this line with a **1/4" "V" gouge** to separate the pants from the stockings.

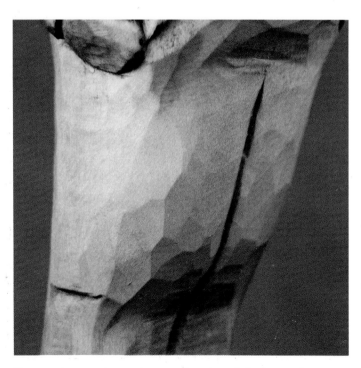

Remove the new sharp edges produced, until the legs and stockings are fairly round.

Then shave *upward* lightly with your knife to blend the stockings into the bottom of the pants.

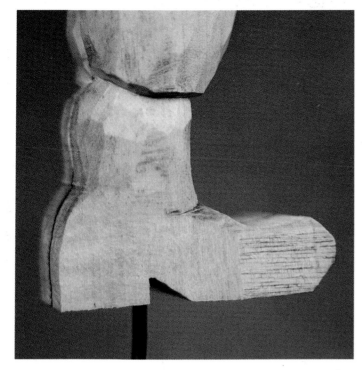

Now scoop away wood from the rear sections of the shoes, using your knife, to make the rear part of the shoes the same thickness as the legs. This will give the front parts of the shoes a nice flare when we are finished.

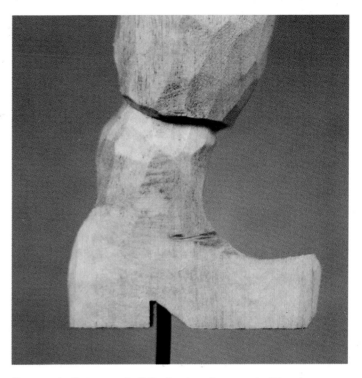

Use your knife to round off the front and rear part of the shoes as shown here...

Here is a view from the bottom.

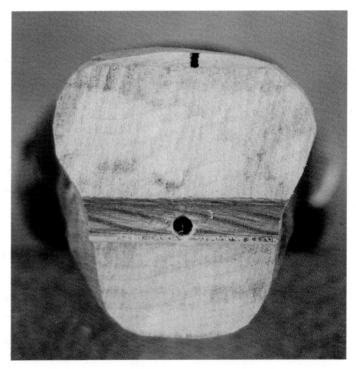

...and again in this bottom view.

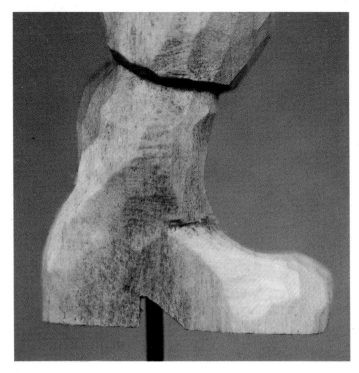

Round off all the sharp edges on the upper part of the shoes, all the way around, using your knife.

...and round off the stockings in the rear.

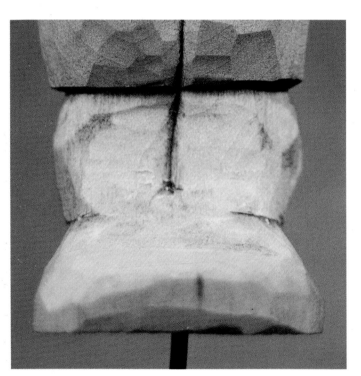

Now round off any sharp edges remaining on the front part of the stockings..

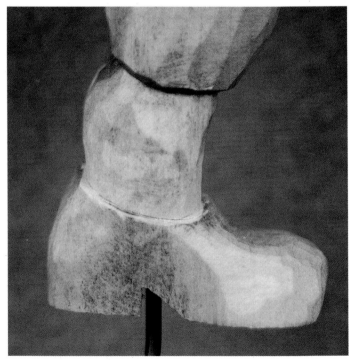

Sketch in some lines to define the shoe and stocking separations. Incise these lines about 1/16" deep with your knife. Shave down from the stockings *toward* the top of the shoes so a small amount of wood is removed. This will give the illusion of the stockings going into the shoes.

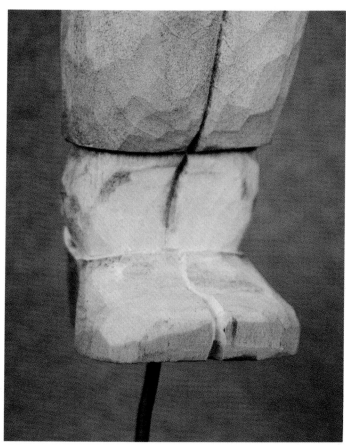

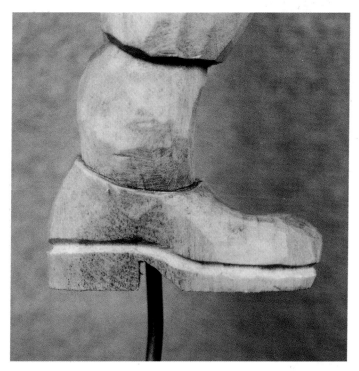

Using a **1/8" "V" gouge,** go around the lower edge of the shoes to define the soles, and separate them from the upper part of the shoes.

Now use a **1/8" "V" gouge** to divide the shoes in front....

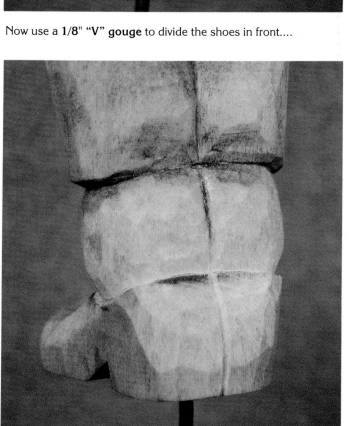

...and in the back.

At this point, we are through with the carving steps. I am going to go ahead and make a base for the elf now, so I can paint and stain everything at one sitting. I used a scrap piece of wood for the base. I normally make the base large enough so that when the carving is centered on it, there is about 3/4" to 1" of excess wood all around. There is no hard, fast rule here. Just make a base that looks good for the size of the carving to be placed on it, yet is large enough to provide stability for the carving.

Painting the Project

Paint the face, lip and hands with FLESHTONE. While the face is still damp, add "blush" to the cheeks, nose and lips using a small amount of BLUSH FLESH blended into the FLESHTONE with a dry brush.

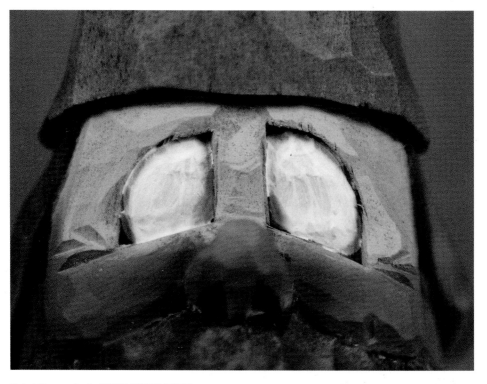

Paint the eyeballs TITANIUM WHITE.

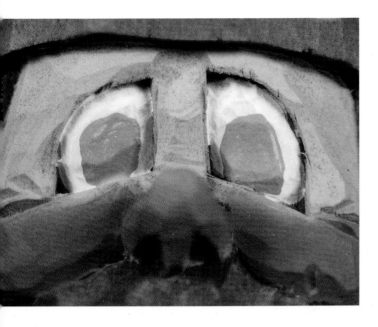

Now take a small, fine-tip brush and put a round dot of BABY BLUE in the center of the eyes.

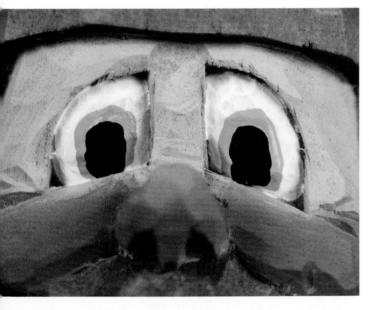

When this is dry, use your fine-tip brush to put a LAMP BLACK dot inside the BLUE dots. The placement of the BLUE and BLACK dots will have various effects on the facial expression. Experiment on a piece of scrap wood to discover all the expressions you can create. I personally like to show the eyes rolled upward, looking toward one side or the other. You may experiment with different looks and find one that you prefer also.

Finally, take a toothpick and put WHITE highlights on the edge of the BLACK dots. If the eyes are looking to the left, I put the highlight around the 10 o'clock position. If looking to the right, I put the highlight around the 2 o'clock position. This is another area you can experiment with on a scrap piece of wood, to see the effects of moving the highlight around.

The beard, hair and eyebrows are painted LIGHT BUTTERMILK. When this is dry, use a dry brush dipped in GREY SKY to lightly go over the high spots of the beard and hair to add a few highlights.

The coat is TRUE BLUE with an EMPEROR'S GOLD button.

The hat is NAPTHOL RED.

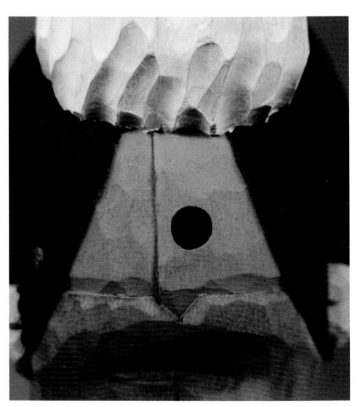

The shirt is YELLOW OCHRE with a LAMP BLACK button.

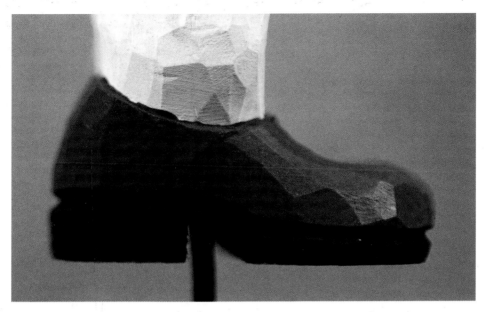

The upper part of the shoes is RED IRON OXIDE, and the soles are BURNT UMBER.

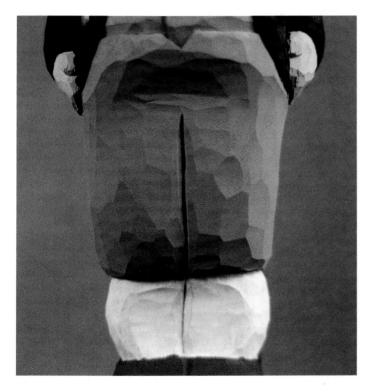

The trousers are MINK TAN and the stockings are TITANIUM WHITE.

Put glue on the bottom of the shoes, and mount the elf to his base. NOTE:Paint or stain the base a color of your choice before gluing the Elf to it.

If you wish to antique and varnish the elf, now is the time to do so. Refer to the section on ANTIQUING for more information.

That's it! We're through for now. Sit back, take a rest, and admire your new creation. I hope you enjoyed this project as much as I did. Until next time...good carving, and please keep those letters and phone calls coming. I really do appreciate hearing from all of you!

Side view of finished project.

Front view of finished project.

Rear view of finished project.

I hope that in some way I have been able to help each of you with some aspect of carving and painting. When we share tips and information, we all become better. If you have any comments or questions about something in this book, or if you have an idea you'd like to see me put in a future book, please feel free to write or call me at the following address and telephone number. I welcome any comments or suggestions you have.

Al Streetman
1609 N. Fordson Drive
Oklahoma City, Ok. 73127
(405) 495-0816

42

Gallery and Study Models

44

45

46

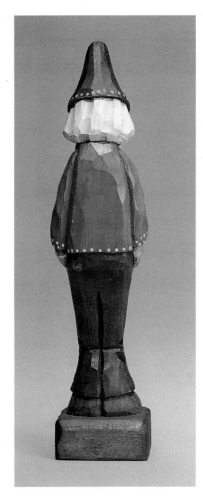

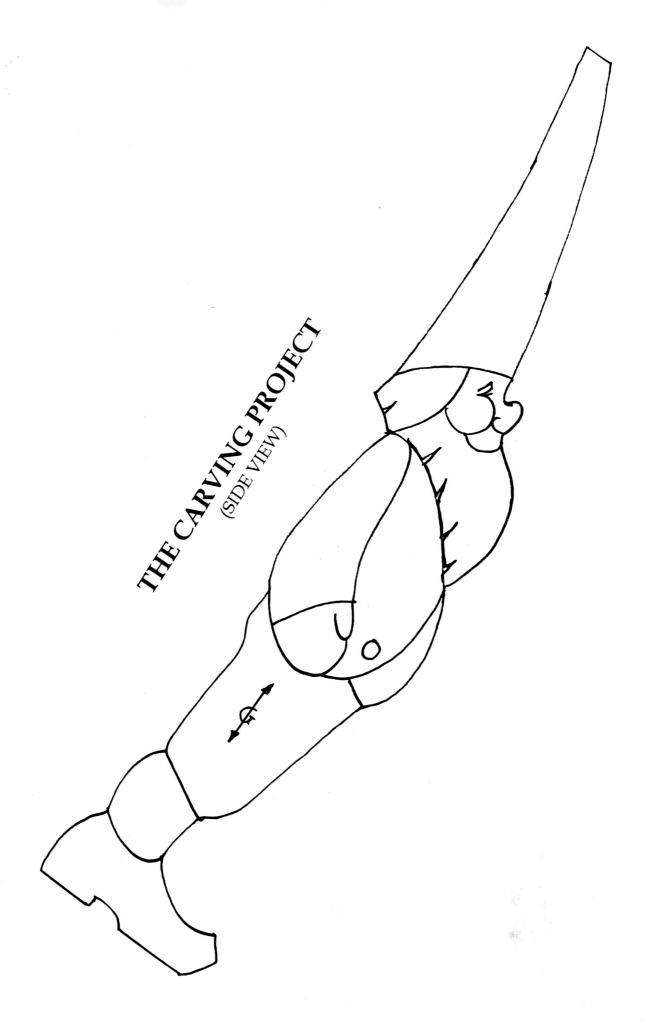

THE CARVING PROJECT
(SIDE VIEW)

THE CARVING PROJECT
(FRONT VIEW)

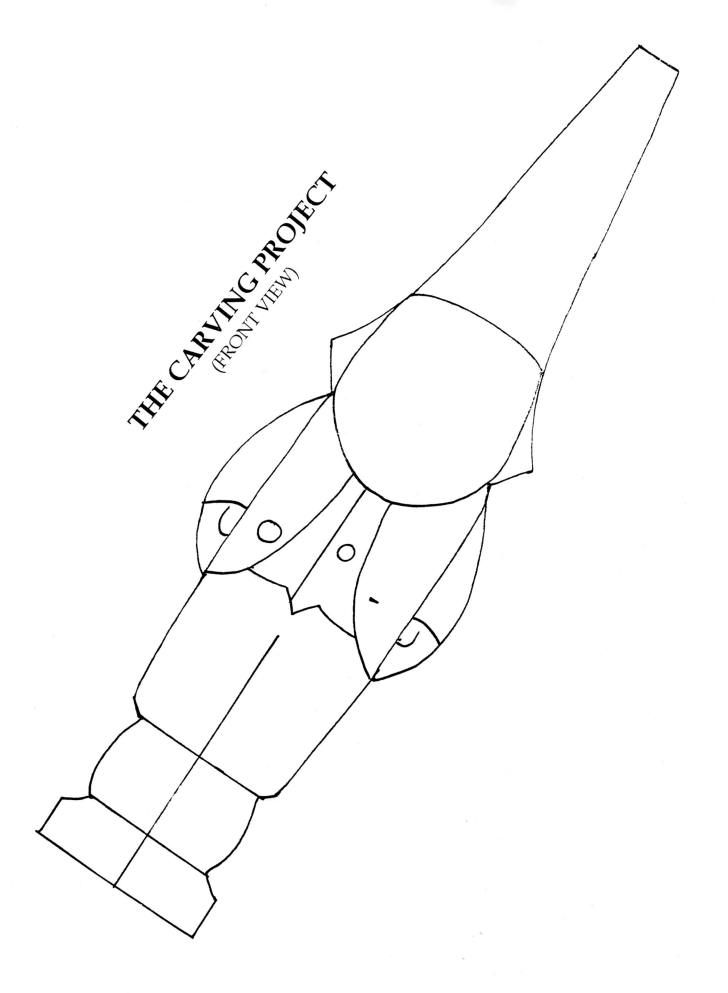

Carve bird separately.
Glue in place after
painting.

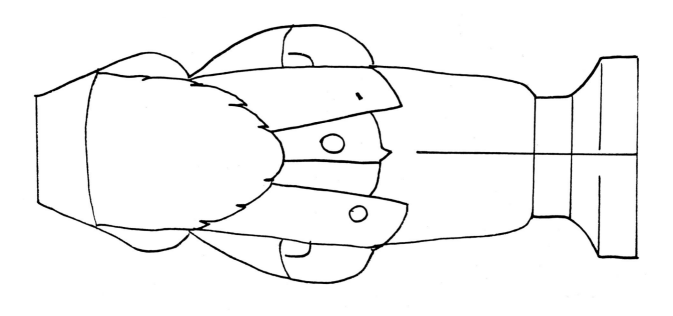

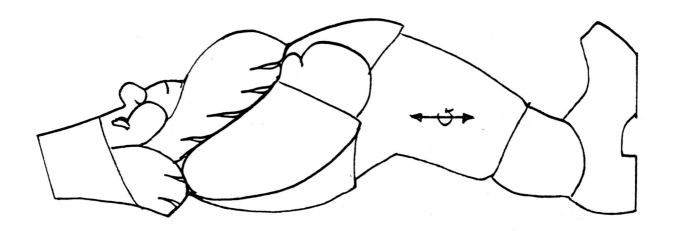

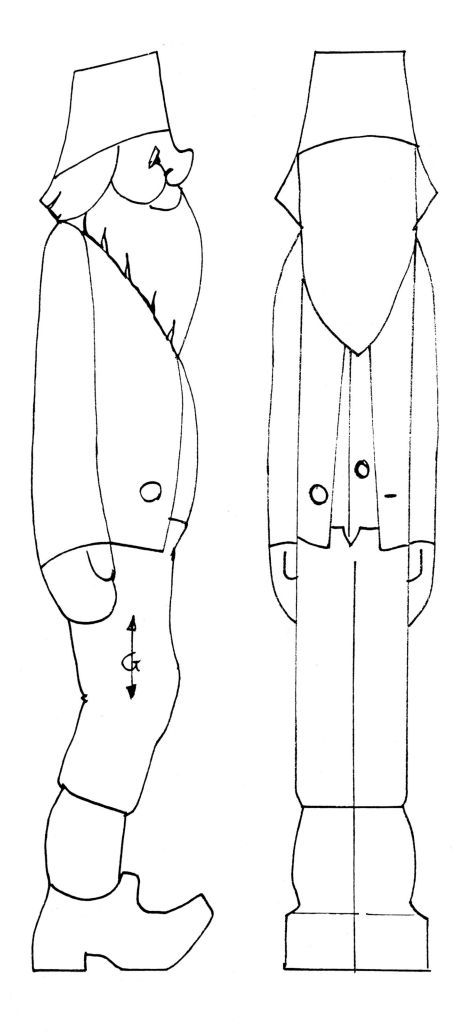

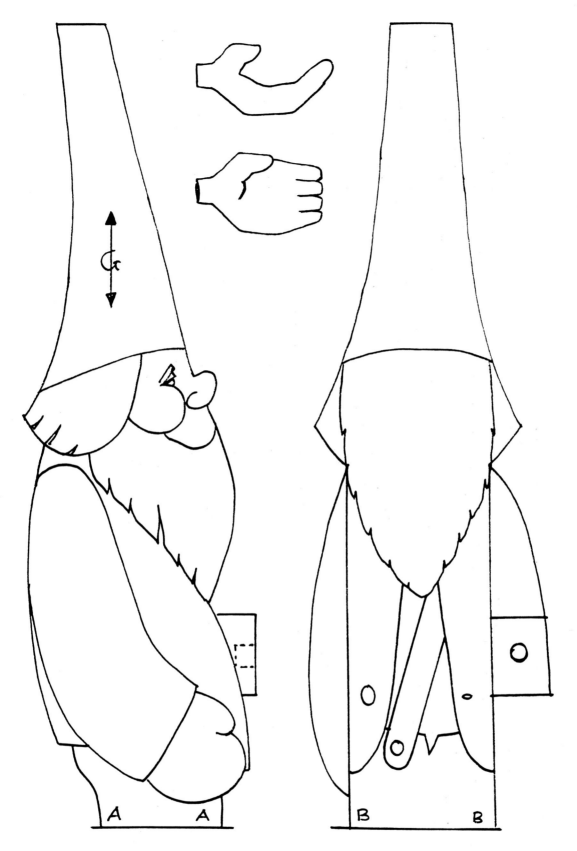

Use this hand for the left hand. Carve the bird separately.
After painting both pieces, glue hand in hole drilled in end
of left arm, then glue bird in place.

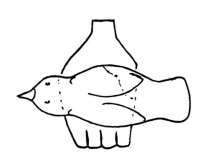
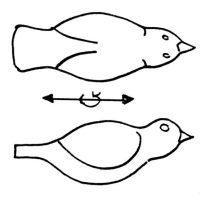

Shape bird so it fits in the
hand.

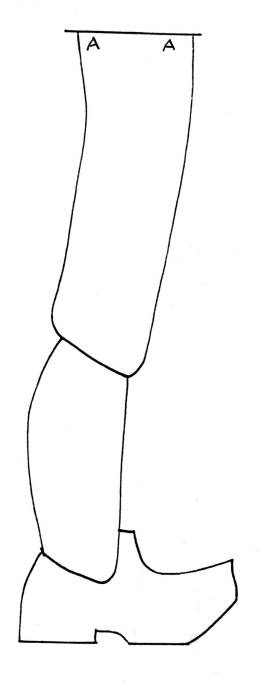

A   A

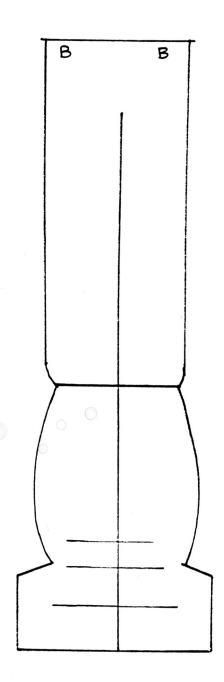

B   B

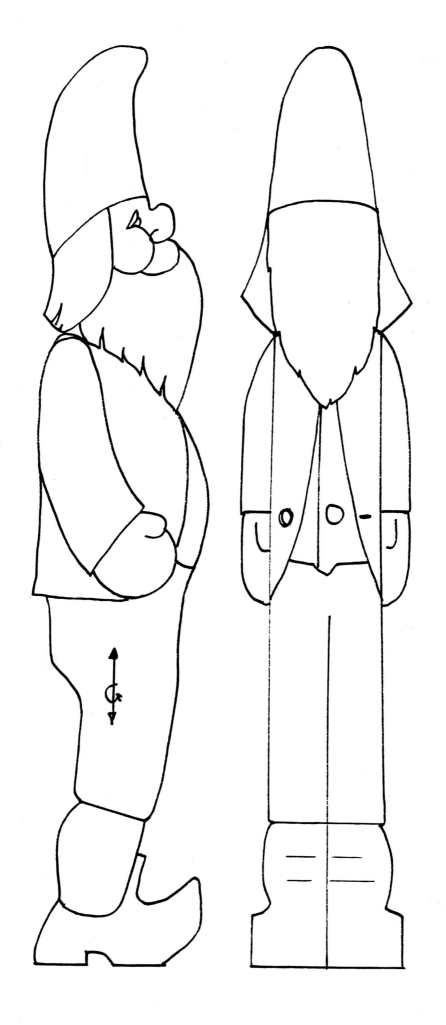

Use this hand for the left hand. Drill hole through hand so the walking stick fits.

Twig, or scrap piece of wood.

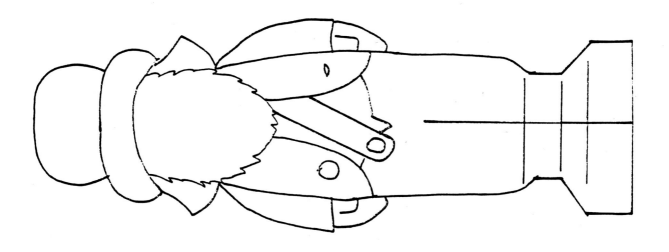

Use this pattern for both hands. Paintbrush and ornament are made from scrap wood. Brush goes through hole in one hand. Attach a small wire to ornament, and attach through other hand.